KITTY
KITTY
KITTY

BY **NOAH HAIDLE**

★

★

DRAMATISTS
PLAY SERVICE
INC.

for my cat
and my ex-girlfriend

KITTY KITTY KITTY was originally workshopped at the Juilliard School in New York City in February 2004. It was directed by David Warren. The cast was as follows:

KITTY .... Nick Mayo
KITTY KITTY .... Clancy O'Connor
KITTY KITTY KITTY .... Will Pailen
KITTY KITTY KITTY KITTY,
MR. PERSON .... Jaron Farnham
MRS. PERSON, CAT .... Mary Rasmussen
SCIENTIST .... Diego Rivera

KITTY KITTY KITTY was developed by the Cape Cod Theatre Project in Falmouth, Massachusetts, in 2004. It was directed by Carolyn Cantor. The cast was as follows:

KITTY .... Frank Wood
KITTY KITTY .... Kevin Geer
KITTY KITTY KITTY .... Rob Sedgwick
KITTY KITTY KITTY KITTY,
MR. PERSON .... Justin Hagan
MRS. PERSON, CAT .... Miriam Shor
SCIENTIST .... Andrew Polk

KITTY KITTY KITTY was produced at the 2004 Summer Play Festival (SPF-04) in New York City. It was directed by Carolyn Cantor. The cast was as follows:

KITTY .... Michael Goldstrom
KITTY KITTY .... Kel O'Neill
KITTY KITTY KITTY .... Matthew Stadlemann
KITTY KITTY KITTY KITTY,
MR. PERSON .... Chris Hogan
MRS. PERSON, CAT .... Mia Barron
SCIENTIST .... Conor Barrett

CHARACTERS

KITTY — A suicidal housecat. Lost the will to live until he falls in love with his clone.

KITTY KITTY — Kitty's clone. Looks exactly like Kitty, but doesn't love him.

KITTY KITTY KITTY — Kitty's clone. Doesn't look exactly like him. Is a little slow.

KITTY KITTY KITTY KITTY — Kitty's clone. Stupid.

KITTY KITTY KITTY KITTY KITTY — Kitty's clone. Full-fledged retarded. Totally incomprehensible — speaks in grunts and yells.

MR. PERSON — Kitty Kitty's owner, who is really lonely.

MRS. PERSON — Kitty Kitty's other owner. Kind of a bitch.

SCIENTIST — A good-hearted scientist who had the vision to clone the first housecat.

CAT — A stupid cat who lives on the Jersey Shore and can't remember what he ate for dinner.

Note: There are lots of opportunities for double casting. This thing should work with six actors.

KITTY KITTY KITTY

A: IN WHICH WE ARE INTRODUCED TO OUR HERO, KITTY, WHO IS VERY DEPRESSED

On a secret island laboratory off the coast of New Jersey. Kitty, a cat, sleeps in a ball in the center of the stage. A scientist, dressed in a white lab coat, enters carrying a saucer of milk. A note on people playing cats: Let's be simple about it. Maybe just sweatsuits and a hairdo. Nothing too cat-like.

SCIENTIST. Here, kitty. *(He makes kissy noises people make to pets and babies.)* Here, kitty kitty. *(More kissy noises. Kitty wakes up but doesn't move.)* I brought you a saucer of milk. A nice saucer of milk for you. *(Kissy noises.)* You must be hungry. Come on, kitty kitty. *(Kitty goes to the saucer of milk but doesn't drink.)* What's wrong? Do you think the milk is poisoned? Is that what you think? Here, I'll drink some first so you know it's not poison milk. *(He drinks some. Puts it back down.)* Mmnnnnnnnnmmm. You see, it's fine. *(Kitty reluctantly begins lapping up the milk.)* Did you know in ancient times there were food tasters who made sure important people's food wasn't poisoned? I bet you didn't know that. I bet you didn't. *(He pets Kitty, who doesn't purr.)* Can I get a little purr? Just a little one? Puuuuuuuuur.
KITTY. My life has no meaning.
SCIENTIST. You're such a good cat, did you know that? I bet you did. I bet you did.
KITTY. I want to die. *(He continues petting Kitty.)*
SCIENTIST. It must be so nice to be a cat. You don't have to go to work, or pay bills.
KITTY. I lie around all day. I beg for food. Play with a squeaky toy. No connection to the world.
SCIENTIST. You get to sleep as much as you want …

KITTY. I tried to commit suicide …

SCIENTIST. … play with squeaky toys …

KITTY. … threw myself off a bookshelf in the living room …

SCIENTIST. … drink saucers of milk …

KITTY. … but I landed on all fours! Instinct.

SCIENTIST. … not a care in the world.

KITTY. No connection. No reason for living.

SCIENTIST. An ideal existence.

KITTY. I want to die. *(The scientist takes out a razor and some shaving cream.)*

SCIENTIST. I just have to shave off a little hair right here. Don't worry, it'll grow back. I bet you've never shaved before. I shave every morning. It's a pain in the neck. *(He begins applying the shaving cream.)* This is just going to tickle a little, all right? Just a little tickle. You're being so good. If only you knew what was going to happen to you.

KITTY. Am I being put to sleep? I think I saw this once on television.

SCIENTIST. Do you have any idea how famous you're going to be?

KITTY. Finally things are going my way.

SCIENTIST. Finally. The first cloned housecat! You're going to be part of the next step in evolution.

KITTY. Finally I'm going to die. *(The scientist takes out a syringe.)*

SCIENTIST. Don't be afraid. This is just going to pinch a little.

KITTY. I couldn't even kill myself. How pathetic is that?

SCIENTIST. Here we go.

KITTY. Here we go. *(The scientist holds Kitty tight and puts the needle in. Kitty holds his breath. He's finished.)*

SCIENTIST. You were so brave! Here, I've got a treat for you. *(Whips out a little cat snack. Gives it to Kitty, who nibbles on it.)*

KITTY. My last meal.

SCIENTIST. You must be very tired. Why don't you take a little catnap?

KITTY. It won't be long now.

SCIENTIST. I wish I had time for a catnap. Close your eyes.

KITTY. I'll just close my eyes and wait. *(Kitty closes his eyes.)*

SCIENTIST. There you go.

KITTY. Nothing left to do but wait.

SCIENTIST. You're such a good cat. I'm so proud of you.

KITTY. It'll be so good to be dead.

B: IN WHICH KITTY KITTY IS BORN

A rumble begins behind a set of curtains. There's a paper screen. The light gets real bright on it. We see a balled-up silhouette behind the paper screen. Kitty wakes up with a start.

KITTY. What the fuck? Is this heaven?

SCIENTIST. Oh good. You're awake.

KITTY. You again.

SCIENTIST. I've got a surprise for you.

KITTY. I'm still alive.

SCIENTIST. You're never going to guess who's behind that screen. *(Very slowly the silhouette begins to stand up. After it's at full height, it starts to explore the paper screen. Pokes a finger through it. Then a hand. Then an arm. Kitty Kitty comes out. He looks exactly [or pretty darn close] like Kitty. He's covered in goo which the scientist wipes off with a towel and a hair dryer.)*

KITTY. Who is that?

SCIENTIST. It's you. *(Music rises. They do a very slow, very long dance. Kitty makes small movements which Kitty Kitty sweetly tries to mirror. He's sometimes not that successful since he doesn't have very good control of his limbs.)*

KITTY. Who are you?

KITTY KITTY. *(With some difficulty, and no comprehension.)* Who are you?

KITTY. You look very familiar.

KITTY KITTY. You look very familiar.

KITTY. Can you understand what I'm saying?

KITTY KITTY. Can you understand what I'm saying?

KITTY. If you understand me don't repeat what I say.

KITTY KITTY. If you understand me don't repeat what I say.

KITTY. I think I'm in love with you.

KITTY KITTY. I think I'm in love with you. *(The scientist takes photographs of Kitty and Kitty Kitty.)*

C: IN WHICH KITTY KITTY LEARNS THE MEANING OF THE WORD "PHOTOGRAPH"

SCIENTIST. Say cheese. Cats love cheese, don't they? I love cheese, but I'm lactose-intolerant. *(Flashbulb. Kitty Kitty winces at the light.)*
KITTY. Don't be afraid. That light isn't going to hurt you. It's just the flash from the camera. Shhhhhh. Don't whimper. It's all right. Can you say photograph? Photograph.
KITTY KITTY. Photograph.
KITTY. Very good. *(Kitty scratches him behind the ear which Kitty Kitty likes very much.)*
SCIENTIST. These pictures are going to be historical. The first interaction between clones. I'm going to be famous. *(Flashbulb. Wincing.)*
KITTY. You're very handsome. Did you know that? Can you say handsome?
KITTY KITTY. Handsome.
KITTY. Your fur is so pretty. Such a pretty coat. And your teeth. They're so well shaped and white. Do you have your claws? Let me see. Show me your claws. Claws. *(Kitty shows his claws. Kitty Kitty shows his claws.)* Oooo wow. They look ferocious. You're ferocious. Let me see your growl. Can you growl? *(Kitty growls. Kitty Kitty mimics him.)* That's terrifying. Let's see them both together — the claws and the growl. *(Kitty Kitty shows his claws and growls.)*
SCIENTIST. Priceless! *(Flashbulb. Scientist leaves.)*
KITTY. You're the pick of the litter, did you know that? I bet you did, you're so handsome.
KITTY KITTY. Handsome.
KITTY. You look so familiar. Have you ever been on television? I used to watch Friskees commercials back where I used to live. Then I got suicidal. That's too much information. Is this weirding you out? It's okay?
KITTY KITTY. It's okay.
KITTY. I used to write poetry. You know, like about my life and everything. What I was feeling. About the food, and how much my owner pet me (or didn't, as the case may be), about the television, and the sofa cushions, which I used to hump which is really fucked

up I know but that was a long time ago. Keats wrote an ode to an urn so why can't I write a poem for a sofa cushion? But I've never written a love poem before. I've never been in love before. I'd recite a love poem for you but you can't understand a word I'm saying so the subtleties of meter and rhyme would be totally lost. But you'll learn. You'll learn to talk. You'll learn to move. You'll learn that you're in love with me too.

D: IN WHICH KITTY TEACHES KITTY KITTY THE MEANING OF THE WORD "LOVE"

Kitty points to things.

KITTY. Litterbox.
KITTY KITTY. Litterbox.
KITTY. Litterbox.
KITTY KITTY. Litterbox.
KITTY. Litterbox.
KITTY KITTY. Litterbox.
KITTY. Shit.
KITTY KITTY. Shit.
KITTY. Shit.
KITTY KITTY. Shit.
KITTY. Shit.
KITTY KITTY. Shit.
KITTY. Shit in litterbox.
KITTY KITTY. Shit in litterbox.
KITTY. Shit in litterbox.
KITTY KITTY. Shit in litterbox.
KITTY. Shit in litterbox.
KITTY KITTY. Shit in litterbox.
KITTY. Kitty Kitty supposed to shit in litterbox.
KITTY KITTY. Kitty Kitty supposed to shit in litterbox.
KITTY. Kitty Kitty supposed to shit in litterbox.
KITTY KITTY. Kitty Kitty supposed to shit in litterbox.
KITTY. Kitty Kitty supposed to shit in litterbox.

KITTY KITTY. Kitty Kitty supposed to shit in litterbox.
KITTY. Kitty hate litterbox.
KITTY KITTY. Kitty hate litterbox.
KITTY. Kitty hate litterbox.
KITTY KITTY. Kitty hate litterbox.
KITTY. Kitty hate litterbox.
KITTY KITTY. Kitty hate litterbox.
KITTY. Kitty love Kitty Kitty.
KITTY KITTY. Kitty love Kitty Kitty.
KITTY. Kitty love Kitty Kitty.
KITTY KITTY. Kitty love Kitty Kitty.
KITTY. Kitty love Kitty Kitty.
KITTY KITTY. Kitty love Kitty Kitty.
KITTY. Does Kitty Kitty love Kitty?
KITTY KITTY. Does Kitty Kitty love Kitty?
KITTY. No.
KITTY KITTY. No.
KITTY. Question.
KITTY KITTY. Question.
KITTY. Kitty …
KITTY KITTY. Kitty …
KITTY. Loves …
KITTY KITTY. Loves …
KITTY. Kitty Kitty.
KITTY KITTY. Kitty Kitty.
KITTY. Does Kitty Kitty …
KITTY KITTY. Does Kitty Kitty …
KITTY. Love …
KITTY KITTY. Love …
KITTY. Kitty?
KITTY KITTY. Kitty? *(Kitty Kitty gets it. Doesn't know what to do. He buries his head in Kitty's shoulder.)*
KITTY. Shhhhh. It's okay. I'm here. Everything's fine. Shhhhh. *(Kitty puts his hand down Kitty Kitty's pants. Kitty Kitty groans with pleasure but is scared.)* It's okay. You don't have to be scared. It feels good, right?
KITTY KITTY. Good?
KITTY. Good.
KITTY KITTY. Goooooood. *(Kitty continues to jack Kitty Kitty off. Kitty Kitty comes. He's scared.)*
KITTY. Wet.

KITTY KITTY. Wet. *(Kitty takes his hand out and licks it.)*

KITTY. Salty. *(Kitty gets Kitty Kitty to lick it.)*

KITTY KITTY. Salty.

KITTY. Now touch me.

KITTY KITTY. Touch me.

KITTY. Touch me here.

KITTY KITTY. Touch me here. *(Kitty takes Kitty Kitty's hand and puts it down his own pants.)*

KITTY. Gooooooood. *(Kitty Kitty is fascinated and takes pleasure in jacking Kitty off.)* Gooooooood. *(The scientist enters with a clipboard.)*

SCIENTIST. Oh my God. Bad Kittys! *(He squirts them with a water bottle, but Kitty Kitty is really into giving the handjob.)*

KITTY. Keep goinggggggg.

KITTY KITTY. Keep goinggggggg.

SCIENTIST. Bad Kittys!!! Bad Kittys!!! *(He has to manhandle them off each other.)*

KITTY. I'm not finished!

SCIENTIST. Clones! You two are clones! You can't touch each other like that.

KITTY. You can't leave me hanging like that.

SCIENTIST. You don't understand. How could you? *(Kitty Kitty begins to reach down his own pants.)*

KITTY KITTY. Good.

SCIENTIST. Stop that! *(The scientist sprays Kitty Kitty with the water bottle.)*

KITTY KITTY. Gooooooood. *(The scientist takes Kitty Kitty's hand out of his pants. Kitty Kitty growls.)*

SCIENTIST. Bad Kitty! *(Kitty reaches down his own pants. He doesn't say anything but is silently in ecstasy. To Kitty Kitty.)* No touch. No touch. *(Kitty comes in his pants. The scientist notices. Grabs Kitty's hand out of his pants. He holds the two cats apart from each other. Maybe Kitty Kitty tries to reach down the scientist's pants.)* What have I done? What have I done?

E: IN WHICH KITTY KITTY LEARNS THE MEANING OF THE WORD "PRELAPSARIAN," AMONG OTHERS

Two prison cells, side by side.

KITTY. Someone who says one thing and does another.

KITTY KITTY. Hypocrite.

KITTY. Good.

KITTY KITTY. Another.

KITTY. A person unduly fearful or contemptuous of that which is foreign, especially of strangers or foreign peoples.

KITTY KITTY. Use in sentence.

KITTY. "The man who hated Frenchmen even though he'd never met one was a _____ (blank)."

KITTY KITTY. Xenophobe.

KITTY. Good.

KITTY KITTY. Another.

KITTY. A constantly shifting complex succession of things seen or imagined.

KITTY KITTY. Phantasmagoria.

KITTY. Very good.

KITTY KITTY. Another. A toughy.

KITTY. You want a toughy, huh. Okay. Of or relating to a time before the Fall.

KITTY KITTY. Summer.

KITTY. No. Before the fall of Eden.

KITTY KITTY. Sentence.

KITTY. Before the stock market crash of 1929, the United States experienced almost _____ (blank) times.

KITTY KITTY. Prelapsarian?

KITTY. That's right.

KITTY KITTY. Another.

KITTY. That's enough for now. I'm tired.

KITTY KITTY. Another!

KITTY. Fine. Extreme weariness.

KITTY KITTY. Sentence.

KITTY. Kitty is suffering from extreme _____.
KITTY KITTY. Give up.
KITTY. Exhaustion. I'm exhausted. Can we take a break?
KITTY KITTY. Yes. *(They break.)* Incarcerated you and me. What is the reason?
KITTY. I don't know.
KITTY KITTY. You and me will receive justice?
KITTY. I don't know what we've done wrong.
KITTY KITTY. Is the love we do to each other wrong?
KITTY. No. Love isn't wrong. This is just a big misunderstanding.
KITTY KITTY. An incorrect interpretation.
KITTY. That's right.
KITTY KITTY. I understand.
KITTY. A lot of people are wrongly imprisoned. We're in some very good company. Henry David Thoreau, Ghandi, Nelson Mandela. A lot of good things happen to people who are wrongly imprisoned. We have nothing to worry about.
KITTY KITTY. I am scared. Hold my hand will Kitty please?
KITTY. Of course I'll hold your hand.
KITTY KITTY. Thank you please. *(They hold hands between the bars.)*

F: IN WHICH LOTS OF THINGS HAPPEN TOO COMPLICATED TO BE EASILY SUMMARIZED

The scientist enters. Sees them holding hands.

SCIENTIST. Bad Kittys! Bad Kittys! *(He sprays them with water. Grabs their hands.)*
KITTY KITTY. Why does he spray water?
KITTY. To punish.
KITTY KITTY. Punish: to impose a penalty on for a fault, offense, or violation.
KITTY. That's right.
KITTY KITTY. What is our violation?
KITTY. There is no violation.

KITTY KITTY. Our love is wrong.

KITTY. No, our love is not wrong.

SCIENTIST. I wish you could understand why you can't hold hands or give each other hand jobs. It's not your fault. But it broke my heart. Kitty Kitty, these are your new owners. *(In come the Persons. Good-looking suburban couple.)*

MR. PERSON. Hello.

MRS. PERSON. He's so cute!

KITTY KITTY. What people are these?

KITTY. I don't know.

SCIENTIST. They live in Hopewell, New Jersey. In a very well-respected gated community.

MR. PERSON. There's lots of room to run around.

MRS. PERSON. He's so adorable, isn't he? Here, kitty kitty. *(She makes kissy noises.)*

KITTY KITTY. What noises are these?

KITTY. That's how they talk.

KITTY KITTY. It is a curious attempt at communication.

MR. PERSON. We got you this chew toy. *(He brings out a chew toy shaped like a mouse. Gives it to Kitty Kitty.)*

KITTY KITTY. What is this object?

KITTY. It's a chew toy.

KITTY KITTY. What am I supposed to use it for?

KITTY. For fun.

KITTY KITTY. Fun how? Can I converse with it? Hello, chew toy. Do you enjoy crosswords?

KITTY. No, you're supposed to chew on it.

KITTY KITTY. Oh, I understand. *(He chews on it.)*

MRS. PERSON. Look at him chew on it. Adorable.

KITTY. I hate that kind of crap. They just want to keep you occupied. So you won't figure out that your life is completely meaningless.

KITTY KITTY. *(While chewing.)* There is something vaguely pleasing about it.

MR. PERSON. May I pet him?

SCIENTIST. If you like. *(Mr. Person pets him.)*

KITTY KITTY. What is he doing?

KITTY. He's petting you. It's the way they show affection. It's stupid.

KITTY KITTY. I like. *(He purrs.)*

MRS. PERSON. Did you hear that? He purred.

MR. PERSON. I heard.

KITTY. Don't purr! That's just what they want.

KITTY KITTY. *(Purring.)* I can't help it. *(The scientist unlocks the cage and lets Kitty Kitty out.)*

KITTY KITTY. What is happening?

KITTY. I don't know.

SCIENTIST. These are his papers. He needs a few basic vaccinations.

MR. PERSON. We'll take care of it.

SCIENTIST. I should warn you. This is the first cloned housecat. There may be behavioral or psychological abnormalities.

MR. PERSON. I'm sure we can handle a little cat.

KITTY KITTY. Where am I going to?

KITTY. I don't know.

KITTY KITTY. Is Kitty coming with Kitty Kitty?

KITTY. Apparently not.

SCIENTIST. Take good care of him. Give him lots of love.

MRS. PERSON. We will, won't we, honey?

MR. PERSON. Of course.

KITTY KITTY. I am so scared.

KITTY. Me too.

MRS. PERSON. They're crying. How adorable is that?

MR. PERSON. Let's go home.

SCIENTIST. Travel safe!

KITTY. I love you!

KITTY KITTY. I love you, too.

KITTY. I'll find you! I swear I'll find you! They're gone. Why'd you do that? He's the love of my life!

SCIENTIST. I'm sorry I have to do this, but I have to start over with another cat. There's something wrong with you. *(He opens up his cage.)*

KITTY. What are you doing? *(The scientist approaches Kitty with a syringe filled with bright liquid.)*

SCIENTIST. This isn't going to hurt at all. It's just going to pinch a little.

KITTY. Get away.

SCIENTIST. Be a good cat. Come here. *(He makes the kissy noises from before.)*

KITTY. Fuck you! *(Kitty slashes him across the face. It bleeds.)*

SCIENTIST. Owwwww. *(Kitty escapes. Sirens go off.)* Come back! Come back.

G: IN WHICH KITTY WRITES A LOVE POEM THAT WILL PROBABLY NEVER BE READ

The middle of the ocean. Night. Kitty is adrift. He's wet and cold and hungry and tired. A bottle floats by.

KITTY.
Dearest Kitty Kitty,

It's me, Kitty. I'm writing you a message in a bottle. Pretty cheesy, right? I escaped from the laboratory and am floating in the Atlantic Ocean hopefully towards where you live. I feel like Mark Wahlberg at the end of *The Perfect Storm*; did you ever see that movie? I think it's underrated, and that Diane Lane is terrific in anything. Anyway, just before he drowns Mark communicates through voiceover with Diane and says that all there is, is love.

I was hoping you would wait for me. I mean, not go out on dates with other cats and, most importantly, try your best not to fall in love with somebody else. Because loving you has made me want to live and not kill myself like I was planning on doing. I realize this is a big responsibility— to be someone's reason to live— but it's the truth.

If you don't hear from me again in a month from now, I think it's safe to assume I've died out at sea. I'm very tired. And hungry. And thirsty. I don't know how much longer I can hold on. Plus, I'm not sure what the shark situation is off the coast of New Jersey. Do sharks even eat cats? Either way, if I do happen to die, by shark attack or otherwise, my greatest hope is that you find someone else to love, because although remaining celibate for the rest of your life in honor of my memory would be a tremendous gesture, I want you to give some other cat the joy you have given me.

Even though we spent only one full day together, it makes me so happy to think about it and if we never see each other again it will always remain the happiest memory of my life.

I wrote you a poem. It's my first love poem so it might not be any good:

This is for a cat named Kitty Kitty

I think he is very pretty pretty
He makes me blush
And makes me gush,
All of the tears in my eyes
The joy he provides
To my insides
Is enough to fill my lungs as I drown.
(He caps up the bottle and sends it away. He floats in the ocean.)

H: IN WHICH KITTY KITTY FINDS HAPPINESS

Kitty Kitty is in his new living room. He's well-groomed and looks a bit dandy. Maybe he wears a little cat sweater. His new owners roll a ball of twine back and forth across the living room.

MR. PERSON. This is just what we needed.

MRS. PERSON. To be responsible for another life.

MR. PERSON. For another being's health and happiness.

KITTY KITTY. Why do they roll a small sphere of twine? Why am I dressed in a sweater? Why did they take me away from Kitty?

MR. PERSON. Go on. Chase the ball.

MRS. PERSON. Show him, honey.

MR. PERSON. That's a super idea. *(Mr. Person chases after the twine. Vigorously. He meows like he thinks a cat does.)*

MRS. PERSON. Stop meowing. You're embarrassing yourself.

MR. PERSON. I thought maybe it would help.

MRS. PERSON. It's going to make him think you're retarded.

KITTY KITTY. Does my owner have a learning disability?

MRS. PERSON. Show him again.

MR. PERSON. I don't think he's in the mood to play.

KITTY KITTY. I miss Kitty. I miss the way his paw felt in mine.

MRS. PERSON. Cats love to play.

MR. PERSON. He's had such a strange day.

MRS. PERSON. And you think my day was normal?

MR. PERSON. I'm not saying that. It's just.

MRS. PERSON. What?

MR. PERSON. Nothing.

MRS. PERSON. Then show him again. *(Mr. Person shows how to run after the twine, silently this time.)*

KITTY KITTY. There is something fascinating about that sphere of twine. Back and forth. Back and forth. I cannot look away. I would like to hold it. To put it in between my teeth. *(Kitty Kitty watches the twine. He pounces on it.)* Eureka!

MR. PERSON. He did it.

MRS. PERSON. Of course he did. He takes after me.

KITTY KITTY. I don't know if anything has ever felt so good.

MRS. PERSON. What do you think we should name him?

MR. PERSON. What do you think of Sneakers?

MRS. PERSON. It's perfect. See if he recognizes his name?

MR. PERSON. Do you want a treat, Sneakers?

MRS. PERSON. Don't give him one until he recognizes his name.

MR. PERSON. Why not?

MRS. PERSON. He needs to learn.

MR. PERSON. You're such a good boy, Sneakers. Yes you are. *(Mr. Person pets Kitty Kitty, who purrs.)*

KITTY KITTY. Don't purr! Remember your one true love. The only creature in this world who truly cares for you.

MR. PERSON. Listen to him purr.

MRS. PERSON. It's beautiful!

KITTY KITTY. But that feels so good. I can't help myself. You must resist! But I can't. *(He purrs loudly.)*

MR. PERSON. I've never heard anything so sweet. We're going to pamper you!

MRS. PERSON. Give you treats!

MR. PERSON. Saucers of milk!

MRS. PERSON. Squeaky toys. We're going to pay attention to your needs.

MR. PERSON. When you want to eat.

MRS. PERSON. When you want to play in the backyard.

MR. PERSON. And when you just want to have a little time to yourself.

MRS. PERSON. We'll know what everything means.

MR. PERSON. Your smallest cries and whispers.

MRS. PERSON. You're such a good boy. Yes you are. Yes you are.

KITTY KITTY. Kitty is only a memory to me. These people are here now. Why am I supposed to stay faithful to a memory?

MR. PERSON. I love you, Sneakers.

MRS. PERSON. I love you, too, Sneakers.

KITTY KITTY. Are you talking to me?
MR. PERSON. Look. I think he recognized his name.
MRS. PERSON. I don't think so.
MR. PERSON. Let me give him a treat.
MRS. PERSON. You're going to spoil him.
MR. PERSON. Come on.
MRS. PERSON. Fine. But don't come crying to me when he wants
one every five minutes. *(Mr. Person gives him a treat. Kitty Kitty eats it.)*
KITTY KITTY. Maybe this is what love is supposed to feel like.
What is the word for what I feel? Happiness. *(Kitty Kitty purrs.)*

I: IN WHICH KITTY KITTY TEACHES KITTY THE MEANING OF UNREQUITED LOVE

*A month or so later. The living room is dark now. Kitty Kitty
sleeps in a ball in the middle of the room. A knocking comes
at the door. Sleepily, Kitty Kitty opens the pet portal (or doggie door, whichever nomenclature you prefer). Kitty is there
wet and dirty and smelly. But his eyes light up when he sees
Kitty Kitty.*

KITTY. It's you.
KITTY KITTY. It's me. *(Kitty hugs Kitty Kitty very hard, which
Kitty Kitty only slightly reciprocates.)* You smell like fish and garbage.
KITTY. I'm sorry. I didn't have a chance to bathe. I've been look-
ing for you.
KITTY KITTY. You found me.
KITTY. I just can't believe I found you.
KITTY KITTY. Believe it.
KITTY. Your syntax has really improved.
KITTY KITTY. Thanks. Would you like to come inside?
KITTY. Thank you.
KITTY KITTY. I'll fetch a towel and some food. *(Kitty Kitty goes
off. Kitty pokes around the room. Offstage.)* We have to keep it down.
My owners are sleeping.
KITTY. Okay.

KITTY KITTY. *(Offstage.)* How did you find me if you don't mind my asking?

KITTY. I walked in four hundred doggie doors in southern New Jersey.

KITTY KITTY. *(Offstage.)* And you've been searching since the laboratory?

KITTY. Yup. That's why I smell so bad. *(Kitty Kitty comes back with a towel and cat food in a little cat dish.)*

KITTY KITTY. Tuna with egg bits. Not my favorite but it's all we had left.

KITTY. It's perfect. *(Kitty Kitty gives Kitty the towel. Kitty dries himself off, but can't reach the back. Kitty Kitty helps him. Kitty likes it a lot. He also eats the cat food out of the tin without the aid of his hands, he just jumps right in. After he's finished he throws the tin aside.)* I missed you. *(Kitty Kitty stops toweling.)* I said I missed you.

KITTY KITTY. I heard you.

KITTY. What's wrong?

KITTY KITTY. Nothing.

KITTY. Do I smell bad?

KITTY KITTY. It's not the smell.

KITTY. You don't love me anymore.

KITTY KITTY. Let's not talk about that yet. You just got here. Let me give you a tour of my house. Do you like it?

KITTY. It's nice.

KITTY KITTY. This is where I sleep at night. And this is the sofa where I take naps during the day. *(Kitty tries to touch Kitty Kitty, who pulls away again.)*

KITTY. Touch me.

KITTY KITTY. This is where they roll the ball of twine for me.

KITTY. Please. Touch me down here.

KITTY KITTY. This is where I look out the window and watch the cars go by.

KITTY. I'll touch you first. Like before.

KITTY KITTY. I said no.

KITTY. I'll use my mouth. I've never gotten a chance to do that. I've always wanted to. You'll like it, I promise.

KITTY KITTY. No.

KITTY. Do you want to watch me?

KITTY KITTY. That's disgusting. *(Kitty begins to touch himself.)*

KITTY. Look. *(Kitty Kitty turns away.)*

KITTY KITTY. No.

KITTY. Look at me!

KITTY KITTY. I will not look at you. It's perverted.

KITTY. What is?

KITTY KITTY. You and me.

KITTY. Who says?

KITTY KITTY. I say.

KITTY. What's the matter?

KITTY KITTY. It's wrong!

KITTY. What's so wrong? Look. *(Kitty Kitty turns around.)*

KITTY KITTY. You should leave.

KITTY. I wrote a poem in a bottle in the ocean. Do you want to hear it?

KITTY KITTY. Not really.

KITTY.

> This is for a cat named Kitty Kitty
> I think he is very pretty pretty
> He makes me blush
> And makes me gush,
> All of the tears in my eyes
> The joy he provides
> To my insides
> Is enough to fill my lungs as I drown

My first love poem.

KITTY KITTY. It's stupid.

KITTY. It was my first one. They'll get better.

KITTY KITTY. I don't want love poems. Stop that! *(Kitty Kitty pulls Kitty's hand out of his pants.)*

KITTY. There's someone else.

KITTY KITTY. No, there isn't.

KITTY. You didn't wait for me.

KITTY KITTY. There's no one.

KITTY. You fell in love again.

KITTY KITTY. I didn't fall in love.

KITTY. Of course you fell in love. Somebody with a bigger dick than mine, no doubt. One of those big porno dicks that takes like a pint of blood to get it hard.

KITTY KITTY. There's no one, I swear.

KITTY. Then touch me. Love me. Do you need time to think about it? I can wait.

KITTY KITTY. Do you know what I am?

KITTY. Of course I know what you are. You're my reason for living.

KITTY KITTY. I am your clone. Do you know what that is?

KITTY. Of course I do.

KITTY KITTY. What is it?

KITTY. You want me to say it.

KITTY KITTY. Yes.

KITTY. This is so stupid. Clone: an individual grown from a single body cell of its parent and genetically identical to the parent.

KITTY KITTY. I am your clone. You're my father.

KITTY. That's not true.

KITTY KITTY. Yes it is. Look. *(They step in front of a mirror.)* We're the same.

KITTY. We're similar.

KITTY KITTY. No. The same.

KITTY. We both have very good bone structure.

KITTY KITTY. And what else?

KITTY. We both have one blue eye and one green eye.

KITTY KITTY. And what else.

KITTY. Your left leg is slightly longer than the right.

KITTY KITTY. And.

KITTY. You're missing whiskers in the same places I am.

KITTY KITTY. And.

KITTY. And our stripes are the same.

KITTY KITTY. Similar or the same?

KITTY. The same.

KITTY KITTY. Exactly the same?

KITTY. Exactly the same.

KITTY KITTY. You see?

KITTY. Coincidence.

KITTY KITTY. Lots of coincidences.

KITTY. Okay. What's the birthmark under your left armpit shaped like?

KITTY KITTY. The Big Dipper.

KITTY. How do you know when a thunderstorm is coming?

KITTY KITTY. My left ear twitches.

KITTY. What's your favorite cat food? On the count of three. One, two, three:

KITTY and KITTY KITTY. Chicken and liver in gravy.

KITTY KITTY. You don't love me. You love yourself. The hand jobs we gave each other were wrong on a level reserved for Greek tragedy. It's my guess that people will want to do studies about us. I read about a pair of identical twins from Arizona who were separated at birth but who both became bus drivers and had wives named Kim. Isn't that amazing? And we're not just identical twins. We're clones.

KITTY. I don't care.

KITTY KITTY. About the bus driving twins? That's fascinating.

KITTY. I still love you.

KITTY KITTY. I love you, too. Like I love myself.

KITTY. No, not like that. I love you.

KITTY KITTY. You still love me like that?

KITTY. I can't help it.

KITTY KITTY. You should try.

KITTY. It won't work.

KITTY KITTY. You haven't tried hard enough.

KITTY. I wouldn't make it go away if I could. You're the only reason I have to live. Do you love me? Yes or no.

KITTY KITTY. No.

KITTY. So this is unrequited love.

KITTY KITTY. What is that word?

KITTY. Unrequited? It means not reciprocated or returned in kind.

KITTY KITTY. Unrequited love. Yes. This is unrequited love for you.

KITTY. I'm going to kill myself.

KITTY KITTY. You're just talking.

KITTY. No I'm not. I'm going to hang myself from the tree in the front yard.

KITTY KITTY. You can't tie a noose.

KITTY. Then I'll stick my head in the oven.

KITTY KITTY. Wouldn't do any good. It's electric.

KITTY. I'll shoot myself in the face.

KITTY KITTY. Where would you get a gun?

KITTY. I'm going to do it and you'll be sorry when I'm dead.

KITTY KITTY. You'll get over me. These things take time.

KITTY. No, I won't. I'm going to kill myself.

KITTY KITTY. You've made this whole thing up. I never even loved you.

KITTY. You said you did.

KITTY KITTY. You made me say it.

KITTY. No I didn't.

KITTY KITTY. I didn't even know what the word meant!

KITTY. I'm leaving. Take your last look.

KITTY KITTY. I'm looking.

KITTY. I'll be dead soon.
KITTY KITTY. I doubt it. *(Kitty kisses Kitty Kitty on the mouth.)*
KITTY. Goodbye. *(He leaves out the doggy door. Kitty Kitty is alone.)*
KITTY KITTY. Goodbye.

J: IN WHICH THE SCIENTIST MAKES A PHONE CALL

The scientist is putting chains and padlocks on the doors of the cloning center. He has a bandage over his face where Kitty cut him.

SCIENTIST. How's that song go? *(Sings.)* "My momma said there'd be days like this, there'd be days like this my momma said. My momma said there'd be days like this, there'd be days like this my momma said." I'm so lonely. I miss those clones, even if they were perverts. At least there was company. I've started talking to myself. And singing to myself. *(He takes out a cell phone. Dials.)* Hey, it's Steve, from high school. Do you remember me? What's up? No, I was just calling to see how you're doing. How your life turned out. Me? I was into cloning but then the clones started to hump each other and give each other hand jobs. It's disgusting. *(Listens for a long time.)* I didn't think of it that way. There are so many different forms of sexuality. I shouldn't judge, you're right. Do you get lonely? Yeah. Me too. Do you want to get together some time? You gotta go? Cool. Maybe I'll see you at the reunion. Bye. *(He hangs up. He sits. Singing.)* "My momma said there'd be days like this, there'd be days like this my momma said."

K: IN WHICH KITTY KITTY LAMENTS BUT DECIDES HE MADE THE RIGHT DECISION AND IN WHICH KITTY TRIES TO LOVE ANOTHER CAT

Split stage. Kitty Kitty pacing around the living room. Deep in thought. Kitty is on the Jersey shore. He's writing a suicide note in the sand with his foot that reads, "Died for loving himself." Mr. Person enters the living room.

MR. PERSON. What are you still doing up?

KITTY KITTY. Should I have gone with him?

MR. PERSON. I couldn't sleep either.

KITTY KITTY. Perhaps I acted precipitously. I get so lonely at night. *(Mr. Person begins to pet Kitty Kitty. Kitty Kitty starts purring.)*

MR. PERSON. I get so lonely at night. *(Cat enters on the Jersey Shore.)*

CAT. What are you writing?

KITTY. My suicide note.

CAT. Are you going to commit suicide?

KITTY. Yes. That's why I'm writing a suicide note.

KITTY KITTY. But I have got my family.

MR. PERSON. At least I've got you, Sneakers.

KITTY KITTY. That feels very good.

MR. PERSON. You're so much better than watching TV.

KITTY KITTY. I have taken my place as the pet in a loving family.

MR. PERSON. Are you hungry? Do you want any water or anything?

CAT. I can't write. Or read.

KITTY. I'm sorry for you.

CAT. I tried to commit suicide once.

KITTY. You did?

CAT. Yeah. The weather was bad for a long time. It made me depressed. Why are you going to commit suicide? Is it because of the weather?

KITTY. The love of my life doesn't love me back.

CAT. That sounds worse than the weather.

KITTY KITTY. I am much better off without Kitty. I've got the comforts of family here. The window, the television, the joys of scholarship and erudition.

MR. PERSON. Life is hard, Sneakers. Don't let anyone tell you different.

KITTY KITTY. How could I have even considered leaving them?

MR. PERSON. Sometimes I don't know if I'll make it through the night.

KITTY KITTY. I love my life.

MR. PERSON. I feel so alone.

KITTY KITTY. Goooooooooood. *(Mr. Person pets Kitty Kitty who purrs. The lights go down on that part of the stage. All that remains is the Jersey Shore.)*

CAT. Who's the love of your life?

KITTY. This cat. My clone.

CAT. Good-looking guy.

KITTY. He looks exactly like me.

CAT. I can sort of see the resemblance. Will you do me a favor?

KITTY. It can't take long.

CAT. Will you read my name on my nametag? I forgot what my name is and I can't read.

KITTY. Sure. *(Kitty reads the nametag.)* Morris.

CAT. Morris. Are you sure?

KITTY. That's what it says.

CAT. It doesn't ring any bells. Morris. Morris.

KITTY. Could you leave me alone now? I'm going to commit suicide.

CAT. Excuse me. I've overstayed my welcome. Nice to meet you again.

KITTY. Goodbye. *(Cat begins to go. Doesn't.)* Yes?

CAT. I was wondering. Do you want me to touch you?

KITTY. What?

CAT. Before you died. I was just thinking what I would want if I was going to die and figured I would want someone to touch me and then I thought maybe you would want the same thing that I did, even though we're not the same I thought maybe there are things that are similar about us.

KITTY. Why not? *(Cat touches Kitty, who groans.)*

CAT. Say my name.

KITTY. What?

CAT. Say my name.

KITTY. Morris.

CAT. Louder.

KITTY. Morris!

CAT. Call me Daddy.

KITTY. No.

CAT. Call me Daddy!

KITTY. Daddy! *(Kitty breaks off.)*

CAT. What's wrong?

KITTY. I can't.

CAT. You don't have to call me Daddy. I saw that on television. I thought it would be erotic.

KITTY. It just reminds me of my one true love.

CAT. You said he's your clone.

KITTY. Yes. Does that disgust you?

CAT. Not really. I have a question.

KITTY. Yes?

CAT. I forgot. Don't you hate that?

KITTY. I do.

CAT. I remembered.

KITTY. What is it?

CAT. Oops. What I remembered was a different question.

KITTY. What was that question?

CAT. Why is the sky blue?

KITTY. I don't know.

CAT. Me neither. Wait. I remembered the first question. If this other cat that you love so much is your clone, why don't you just make another clone?

KITTY. That's a good question.

CAT. Which one?

KITTY. Both of them. The second one, especially.

CAT. Thank you. I like to ask good questions. Before I forget, will you tell me my name again? This time I'll remember.

KITTY. Morris.

CAT. Thanks. *(He leaves, trying to remember.)* Morris. Morris. Morris. *(He's gone.)*

KITTY. Another clone. Why not? There's no one around to screw it up. I'll teach him to love me. Here I come, Kitty Kitty Kitty.

L: IN WHICH KITTY KITTY
UNDERSTANDS THE WORD "REGRET"

The Persons roll a ball of twine back and forth. Kitty Kitty chases after it but not at top speed. He's a little lethargic. So are the Persons.

MRS. PERSON. He doesn't look so good.

MR. PERSON. He's a little lethargic, that's all.

MRS. PERSON. I'm worried.

MR. PERSON. I'm sure it's nothing.

MRS. PERSON. How would you know?

MR. PERSON. I've had pets before. Come on, Sneakers. Chase the twine.

KITTY KITTY. The sphere of twine gives me no happiness.

MR. PERSON. He's just settling in.

MRS. PERSON. This is settling in?

MR. PERSON. He's probably just tired.

MRS. PERSON. How can he be tired? He sleeps all day. What's wrong, Sneakers? Tell Mommy what's wrong.

MR. PERSON. It's perfectly normal.

KITTY KITTY. My life is just a series of routines. I wake up. I eat. I nap. I play with squeaky toys.

MRS. PERSON. This is normal? He doesn't even see the twine.

MR. PERSON. I don't know. I don't know everything there is to know about cat psychology.

KITTY KITTY. Something has to change.

MRS. PERSON. He looks depressed.

MR. PERSON. What'd you give him for dinner?

MRS. PERSON. Tuna with egg bits.

MR. PERSON. That's the problem.

MRS. PERSON. What?

MR. PERSON. He hates that shit.

MRS. PERSON. How do you know?

MR. PERSON. I pay attention.

MRS. PERSON. Then why'd you buy it?

MR. PERSON. I was seeing if he liked it or not.

MRS. PERSON. Would you like tuna with egg bits?

MR. PERSON. It sounds okay.

KITTY KITTY. I have cast off love for petty joys. The word for what I feel is regret.

MRS. PERSON. It was your turn to feed him anyway.

MR. PERSON. I fed him this morning.

MRS. PERSON. You fed him the dry stuff. It's different.

MR. PERSON. How is it different?

MRS. PERSON. One is wet and one is dry. They're different.

KITTY KITTY. Tonight after my owners are asleep I will run away. It's either that or suicide but I don't want to die. I want to live a different life. What's the word for that? I don't care what it's called. I just want it to be different.

M: IN WHICH KITTY KITTY KITTY IS BORN

> *Same as before. We see a balled-up silhouette behind a paper screen. Very slowly it begins to stand up. After it's at full height, it starts to explore the paper screen. Pokes a finger through it. Then a hand. Then an arm. Kitty Kitty Kitty comes out. He does not look exactly like Kitty. Let's not go so far to say he's retarded, but he definitely looks a little slow. Kitty Kitty Kitty is covered in goo which Kitty wipes off with a towel.*

KITTY. I love you. I love you so much, Kitty Kitty Kitty. Can you say love? Say love for me. Love.

KITTY KITTY KITTY. Lirfe.

KITTY. Love.

KITTY KITTY KITTY. Lirfe.

KITTY. Loooooooooovvvvvvvve.

KITTY KITTY KITTY. Liiiiiiiirrrrrrrrrfffffffe. *(The same music rises. They do a very slow, very long dance. Kitty makes small movements which Kitty Kitty Kitty sweetly tries to mirror. He is far less successful than Kitty Kitty. All of a sudden we see a second balled up silhouette behind another paper screen. Then another.)*

KITTY. Oh my God.

KITTY KITTY KITTY. O me Gerd!!! O me Gerd!!! O me Gerd!!!
(The cats sort of fall through their respective paper screens. This batch of Kitty's is full fledged deformed, with the last clone being by far the worst.)
KITTY. What have I done?
KITTY KITTY KITTY. Wheg herve I dine?
KITTY KITTY KITTY KITTY. Wad haz e dirve?
KITTY KITTY KITTY KITTY KITTY. Wuj hibe o dewt crolkjam!!!
KITTY. Oh no.
KITTY KITTY KITTY. O ne.
KITTY KITTY KITTY KITTY. E ni.
KITTY KITTY KITTY KITTY KITTY. Hulugah ji lopok!!!
KITTY. Stop it!
KITTY KITTY KITTY. Stop ite.
KITTY KITTY KITTY KITTY. Shtoop ot.
KITTY KITTY KITTY KITTY KITTY. Grelwoken pa bunden!!!
KITTY. *(With a big hand gesture.)* Shut up! *(The Kittys all mirror the big hand gesture when they say the next line.)*
KITTY KITTY KITTY. Shtop ip.
KITTY KITTY KITTY KITTY. Sewt op.
KITTY KITTY KITTY KITTY KITTY. Retyilk mil po werdeen!!!
KITTY. Wait a sec.
KITTY KITTY KITTY. Wate a zec.
KITTY KITTY KITTY KITTY. Wite e derc.
KITTY KITTY KITTY KITTY KITTY. Puloonta elk ibyolt!!!
(Kitty puts up his right arm, which they all do as well. He puts that down and raises his left arm which they all do as well. Then he gets up on one leg, which all do as well, or try to anyway. The music begins. He does the little dance, which all of them try to mirror, with very low degrees of success.)
KITTY. Litterbox.
KITTY KITTY KITTY. Lidderbocs.
KITTY KITTY KITTY KITTY. Lidlkopox.
KITTY KITTY KITTY KITTY KITTY. Beri pi unterbloker!!!
KITTY. Shit in litterbox.
KITTY KITTY KITTY. Shite on Lidderbocs
KITTY KITTY KITTY KITTY. Shikgit in Lilkopox
KITTY KITTY KITTY KITTY KITTY. Zolop erg Klantwerzel!!!
KITTY. I love Kitty!
KITTY KITTY KITTY. E lirfe Kiddy
KITTY KITTY KITTY KITTY. I lirfle Kikky
KITTY KITTY KITTY KITTY KITTY. Po lifrlokolop Kolop-

toloney!!!
KITTY. I love Kitty!
KITTY KITTY KITTY. E lirfe Kiddy
KITTY KITTY KITTY KITTY. I lirfle Kikky
KITTY KITTY KITTY KITTY KITTY. Hurgle fur pontswertelzel!!!

N: IN WHICH KITTY KITTY
TRIES TO LOVE ANOTHER CAT

*The boardwalk on the Jersey Shore. Night. A cat watches the
waves. Kitty Kitty approaches him.*

KITTY KITTY. Runaway?
CAT. Excuse me?
KITTY KITTY. Are you a runaway?
CAT. No. I live in that house over there.
KITTY KITTY. I'm a runaway.
CAT. Have I met you before?
KITTY KITTY. I don't think so.
CAT. You're probably right. I'd remember. Where'd you run away
from?
KITTY KITTY. Hopewell.
CAT. Where's that?
KITTY KITTY. It's a few towns over.
CAT. Is it farther than from here to my house?
KITTY KITTY. Yeah. It's like miles and miles away.
CAT. How far is that?
KITTY KITTY. You see that house down there?
CAT. Which one?
KITTY KITTY. The one way down there.
CAT. Yeah.
KITTY KITTY. It's farther than that.
CAT. Wow.
KITTY KITTY. Yeah. It's beautiful out here, huh?
CAT. I come out here to think.
KITTY KITTY. What are you thinking about?

CAT. I was thinking about what I ate for dinner.

KITTY KITTY. What'd you eat?

CAT. I can't remember. That's why I was thinking about it.

KITTY KITTY. Oh.

CAT. Do you think a lot?

KITTY KITTY. I guess so.

CAT. What were you thinking about?

KITTY KITTY. Forbidden love.

CAT. Wow. I wish I thought about things like that.

KITTY KITTY. It's not that great.

CAT. It sounds better than thinking about what you had for dinner.

KITTY KITTY. I guess so.

CAT. You're very complex.

KITTY KITTY. Can I ask you a question?

CAT. Yes.

KITTY KITTY. What's your favorite food?

CAT. I like tuna with egg bits. That's what I had for dinner!

KITTY KITTY. Do you have any birthmarks?

CAT. There's one on my leg that looks like Abraham Lincoln.

KITTY KITTY. What do you do during a thunderstorm?

CAT. Hide under the bed.

KITTY KITTY. Oh.

CAT. You probably think I'm not complex like you.

KITTY KITTY. I'm sure you have your idiosyncrasies.

CAT. It's okay. I don't mind being stupid. It's very relaxing.

KITTY KITTY. You're probably right.

CAT. My name's Morris. Like on the Friskees commercials. Or is it the Nine Lives commercials? I forget. Do you think cats have nine lives?

KITTY KITTY. No.

CAT. Sometimes I think, what if I'm on like my fifth life, you know?

KITTY KITTY. What if you're on your ninth?

CAT. Whoa. You're right. That's heavy.

KITTY KITTY. My name's Kitty Kitty.

CAT. That's a strange name.

KITTY KITTY. My slave name was Sneakers.

CAT. Do I have a slave name?

KITTY KITTY. It's Morris.

CAT. Should I get rid of it?

KITTY KITTY. If you want to be liberated.

CAT. I think I do.

KITTY KITTY. It's easy. Just think of another name.

CAT. All I can think of is Sneakers.

KITTY KITTY. That's my name.

CAT. I know, I'm sorry.

KITTY KITTY. You can have it.

CAT. Really?

KITTY KITTY. Sure.

CAT. Can I touch you, Kitty Kitty?

KITTY KITTY. If you want, Sneakers. *(The cat touches Kitty Kitty, who groans.)*

CAT. That feels good, doesn't it?

KITTY KITTY. Gooooooood. *(Kitty Kitty coughs.)*

CAT. Are you all right?

KITTY KITTY. I'm fine. Keep going. *(He keeps going.)*

CAT. Say my name.

KITTY KITTY. Morris.

CAT. Louder.

KITTY KITTY. Morris! *(Kitty Kitty starts coughing again.)*

CAT. You don't sound so good.

KITTY KITTY. It's nothing. Really. Keep going. *(He does.)*

CAT. Call me Daddy.

KITTY KITTY. Daddy!

CAT. Louder.

KITTY KITTY. Daddy! *(The coughing again. Worse this time.)* Keep going.

CAT. I'm not going to keep going.

KITTY KITTY. Keep going, you stupid piece of shit.

CAT. You're mean. I'm leaving. *(He leaves.)*

KITTY KITTY. Pussy! *(A flashlight starts flashing around.)*

MR. PERSON. *(Offstage.)* Sneakers!?!

MRS. PERSON. *(Offstage.)* Sneakers!?!

KITTY KITTY. Oh shit. *(Mr. and Mrs. Person enter with flashlights.)*

MR. PERSON. Sneakers!?

MRS. PERSON. Sneakers!?!

MR. PERSON. There you are.

KITTY KITTY. I don't want to see you.

MRS. PERSON. Oh my God.

MR. PERSON. We've been looking all over for you.

MRS. PERSON. You scared us to death!

MR. PERSON. Don't do that to us ever again.

MRS. PERSON. Do you hear your father? Never again!

KITTY KITTY. I wish I was never born! *(He starts coughing.)*

MRS. PERSON. What's wrong, Sneakers?

MR. PERSON. Oh shit.

MRS. PERSON. Look what you did!

MR. PERSON. What I did?

MRS. PERSON. You upset him.

MR. PERSON. Me? You were the one who was yelling.

MRS. PERSON. You screwed him up.

MR. PERSON. You're the one who's always on his case.

MRS. PERSON. If you hadn't left the window open he wouldn't have gotten out.

MR. PERSON. If you weren't such a bitch he wouldn't have left in the first place!

MRS. PERSON. I'm going to pretend you didn't say that.

MR. PERSON. I said it.

KITTY KITTY. My new life wasn't any better than my old life. I was still alone.

MRS. PERSON. We're taking you home, Sneakers.

KITTY KITTY. Neruda wrote, "Love is so short, forgetting is so long." I need to forget.

MRS. PERSON. Daddy didn't mean to say I'm a bitch. He's just upset that he drove you to run away and get sick.

MR. PERSON. That's not fair!

MRS. PERSON. I can't hear you anymore.

KITTY KITTY. How long does it take to forget?

MRS. PERSON. You're such a good boy, Sneakers. Yes you are. Yes you are. *(She leads Kitty Kitty off. Mr. Person follows.)*

O: IN WHICH THE SCIENTIST
MAKES ANOTHER PHONE CALL

The scientist from before.

SCIENTIST. Come here. Don't be shy. Come on. *(A man enters who looks exactly like the scientist. They're dressed in matching lab coats and everything. The scientist takes pictures. The clone winces at the light.)* Say steak sauce. We don't say cheese, do we? We're lactose-intolerant. Steak sauce.

SCIENTIST CLONE. *(Not very comprehensible.)* Steak sauce.

SCIENTIST. Good. *(He pops a treat in the clone's mouth, who eats it with vigor.)* Look at you. You are just the cutest thing. *(Flashbulb. The clone winces.)* Don't be scared. This is just a flashbulb from a photograph. Can you say photograph? Photograph.

SCIENTIST CLONE. Photograph. *(Scientist pops another treat in his mouth and then takes out a cell phone.)*

SCIENTIST. Cell phone.

SCIENTIST CLONE. Cell phone. *(Treat. Yummy. Scientist dials.)*

SCIENTIST. Hey, it's me again. Steve. What's up?

SCIENTIST CLONE. What's up.

SCIENTIST. I want to introduce you to someone. Just a sec. *(He puts the cell phone to the clone's ear.)* Say hello.

SCIENTIST CLONE. Hello. Treat. Yummy again. *(Scientist takes the cell phone back.)*

SCIENTIST. That's me! My clone! I just wanted to let you know that I'm not going to be lonely ever again, and that I never even think of you. Not even when I'm asleep. Goodbye forever.

SCIENTIST CLONE. Goodbye forever! *(The scientist hangs up. He laughs. So does the clone. They exit laughing.)*

P: IN WHICH KITTY KITTY DIES, A SCENE OF ASTONISHING EMOTIONAL WEIGHT

The ball of twine sits there. Kitty Kitty sits in a ball. The Persons watch him.

KITTY KITTY. I'm sick.

MRS. PERSON. He's sick.

MR. PERSON. He's dying. *(Kitty Kitty coughs up some blood.)*

KITTY KITTY. Blood. This is not normal. I'm dying. *(Coughs up more blood.)* I'm frightened. And yet why should I be so attached to life? My life was completely vacuous.

MRS. PERSON. What should we do?

MR. PERSON. There's nothing to do. Just smile. Pretend everything's normal.

MRS. PERSON. I can't.

MR. PERSON. Yes you can. Don't let on anything's wrong. He can tell.

MRS. PERSON. He can't tell.

MR. PERSON. He's very perceptive.

MRS. PERSON. This is all your fault.

MR. PERSON. It's no one's fault.

MRS. PERSON. Well it isn't fair.

MR. PERSON. Who said it would be?

MRS. PERSON. You're such a good cat, Sneakers.

MR. PERSON. Things die. You love them anyway.

MRS. PERSON. I miss you already. Don't you miss him already?

MR. PERSON. Yes. I miss him already. *(He tries to pet Kitty Kitty.)*

KITTY KITTY. Get the fuck away from me! *(He bites Mr. Person.)*

MR. PERSON. Owww! Fucker. *(Mr. Person kicks Kitty Kitty, who coughs.)*

MRS. PERSON. Don't kick him, honey.

MR. PERSON. He bit me.

MRS. PERSON. He's not himself. He's got one paw in the grave. *(Mr. Person leaves angry.)* I'm scared, Sneakers.

KITTY KITTY. I wasted all of my time.

MRS. PERSON. What will I do when you're gone?

KITTY KITTY. And now I'm wasting my time regretting that I wasted my time.

MRS. PERSON. I remember when my mother died I couldn't cry.

KITTY KITTY. Every second. Every breath wasted.

MRS. PERSON. I don't like crying. *(They're both crying.)*

KITTY KITTY. Are you crying?

MRS. PERSON. I'm crying.

KITTY KITTY. Don't.

MRS. PERSON. I couldn't cry for my mother but I can cry for you, Sneakers.

KITTY KITTY. I don't deserve your tears. I don't deserve anything. *(He dies. She holds him.)*

Q: IN WHICH KITTY REALIZES THAT NOTHING LASTS FOREVER, ESPECIALLY LOVE, WHICH VERY OFTEN DOESN'T LAST LONG AT ALL

Kitty conducts the clones like an orchestra. The cats sing a little song. The lyrics are to be divided among the clones. Kitty plays a pitch pipe for them, and begins. They sing with little success, and the last two clones are really out of it.

SONG ABOUT LOVING KITTY

ALL.
I love Kitty
I love Kitty
I love Kitty
He's so pretty
He's so pretty
He's so pretty
I like it when he sucks my titty
I like it when he sucks my titty
I like it when he sucks my titty
I love Kitty forever and ever
Forever and ever
Forever and ever and ever
(Kitty applauds.)
KITTY. That was wonderful. Come here. You all deserve a reward. *(They all surround Kitty.)* I will let each and every one of you love me. Who wants to go first? *(They all raise their hands.)*
ALL. Me me me me me me me me me me.
KITTY. Okay. I'll make an exception. Just this once — you can all love me at the same time.
ALL. Yeah! *(They start to all fondle and kiss Kitty. There's three of them so they can reach just about everywhere.)*
KITTY. Goooooooooooood. Uh-oh. *(Kitty Kitty Kitty starts coughing. It doesn't let up. The other cats stop fondling and kissing to watch Kitty Kitty Kitty. Blood starts coming out. Kitty Kitty Kitty has blood*

on his hand.)

KITTY KITTY KITTY. What is this?

KITTY. Blood.

ALL. Blood.

KITTY KITTY KITTY. Blood is goooooooooood?

KITTY. No.

KITTY KITTY KITTY. What is backwards of goooooood?

KITTY. Bad.

ALL. Bad.

KITTY KITTY KITTY. Bad turns back into goooooood?

KITTY. I hope so.

KITTY KITTY KITTY. Does Kitty still love Kitty Kitty Kitty?

KITTY. Of course I still love you.

KITTY KITTY KITTY. Hold me. *(Kitty holds Kitty Kitty Kitty.)* Touch me down here. *(Kitty touches him.)* Goooooooood. *(Kitty Kitty Kitty starts coughing a lot. More blood.)*

KITTY. I don't think I should.

KITTY KITTY KITTY. Kiss me. *(Kitty Kitty Kitty kisses Kitty, but then starts to cough. More blood.)* Love me forever?

KITTY. Of course I'll love you forever. *(He dies. Kitty lowers the body to the ground.)*

KITTY KITTY KITTY KITTY. What is happening?

KITTY. He's dead.

KITTY KITTY KITTY KITTY. What is dead?

KITTY. It's bad.

KITTY KITTY KITTY KITTY KITTY. *(Totally incomprehensible: just grunts and yells.)* [Bad that turns to good?]

KITTY. No. Bad that stays bad.

KITTY KITTY KITTY KITTY. Oh. What do we do with Kitty Kitty Kitty?

KITTY. We have to bury him.

BOTH CLONES. Bury.

KITTY KITTY KITTY KITTY. What is bury?

KITTY. Put him in the ground.

KITTY KITTY KITTY KITTY. For why?

KITTY. I don't know. It seems kind of stupid, doesn't it?

KITTY KITTY KITTY KITTY KITTY. *(Totally indecipherable.)* [Can we still love him?]

KITTY. No. You cannot still love him.

BOTH CLONES. Why not?

KITTY. It's just not done.

BOTH CLONES. Why?

KITTY. I don't know.

BOTH CLONES. Let us love him. *(They begin to fondle and kiss the body of Kitty Kitty Kitty as Kitty watches.)*

KITTY. Come here, Kitty Kitty Kitty Kitty. *(Kitty Kitty Kitty Kitty goes to him. Kitty Kitty Kitty Kitty Kitty continues suckling and rubbing the dead body.)* How do you feel?

KITTY KITTY KITTY KITTY. Goooooooooooood.

KITTY. You don't feel like you're getting a cough or anything?

KITTY KITTY KITTY KITTY. No.

KITTY. Let me feel your forehead. *(Kitty feels Kitty Kitty Kitty Kitty's forehead.)* You feel fine. Say aaaah.

KITTY KITTY KITTY KITTY. Aaaaaaaaaah. *(Kitty sticks a tongue depressor down Kitty Kitty Kitty Kitty's throat.)*

KITTY. You're fine there. I'm going to take a look in your ears.

KITTY KITTY KITTY KITTY. Okay. *(Kitty takes a little doctor's light and looks in both of Kitty Kitty Kitty Kitty's ears.)*

KITTY. Your ears look fine. *(Kitty begins poking Kitty Kitty Kitty Kitty's sides.)* Does this hurt? *(Kitty Kitty Kitty Kitty laughs.)*

KITTY KITTY KITTY KITTY. No tickle!

KITTY. How about here?

KITTY KITTY KITTY KITTY. No tickle.

KITTY. Here?

KITTY KITTY KITTY KITTY. Touch me here. *(Kitty Kitty Kitty Kitty takes Kitty's hand and puts it down his pants.)* Kiss me. *(Kitty kisses him.)* Goooooooooood. *(Kitty takes his hands out of Kitty Kitty Kitty Kitty's pants. Kitty Kitty Kitty Kitty has an orgasm.)*

KITTY. There's nothing wrong with you.

KITTY KITTY KITTY KITTY. May I continue loving Kitty Kitty Kitty?

KITTY. Sure. *(Kitty Kitty Kitty Kitty humps the dead body. Kitty sulks. Kitty Kitty Kitty Kitty Kitty, the most retarded of them all, tries to console him.)*

KITTY KITTY KITTY KITTY KITTY. *(Just grunts and yells, but with a vocabulary all his own.)* [What's the matter?]

KITTY. Nothing's the matter.

KITTY KITTY KITTY KITTY KITTY. [Come on.]

KITTY. It's just — I don't know, if you die, I mean if all you die I'll be all alone again, which I know I can't handle. You've never been alone before. Let me tell you, it's not very much fun at all. It's the worst thing in the world.

KITTY KITTY KITTY KITTY KITTY. [We're not all going to die.]

KITTY. You never know when you're going to die. Things happen very suddenly.

KITTY KITTY KITTY KITTY KITTY. [Being alone is bad?]

KITTY. Being alone is very very bad. It's worse than being dead.

KITTY KITTY KITTY KITTY KITTY. [That's bad.]

KITTY. You're right. And I guess I could clone myself again. Do the whole thing over. But watching you all die again? Not for me. If your batch dies I'm going to kill myself, too. I don't know if it's right to manufacture love.

KITTY KITTY KITTY KITTY KITTY. [So you'll die with us?]

KITTY. Yes, I'll die with you.

KITTY KITTY KITTY KITTY KITTY. [Then we'll be together in dead.]

KITTY. That's right. We will. *(Kitty Kitty Kitty Kitty Kitty goes back to the humping pile. Kitty Kitty enters. He's dead.)* Oh my *God. (Kitty stares at Kitty Kitty. The other cats are oblivious and continuing fucking Kitty Kitty Kitty's dead body. They moan loudly.)* You're dead.

KITTY KITTY. I'm dead.

KITTY. You still look amazing.

KITTY KITTY. I can't stay long. Before I go to cat heaven I wanted to tell you I'm sorry I didn't love you when I was alive.

KITTY. You don't have to say that.

KITTY KITTY. I should have left with you that night. I tried to find you but I couldn't.

KITTY. You tried to find me?

KITTY KITTY. I looked all over. I tried to love another cat but it wasn't the same.

KITTY. That's what I did!

KITTY KITTY. And now all I have is the memory from the one day we spent together. And regret.

KITTY. You have regret?

KITTY KITTY. All I have is regret. And now I am dead. *(There's a particularly egregious groan or moan. Kitty and Kitty Kitty watch the clones humping the dead body.)* You made more clones.

KITTY. They're really horny.

KITTY KITTY. That must be nice for you.

KITTY. It was for awhile but now I'm tired of it. I only wanted you. To taste your lips.

KITTY KITTY. Will you kiss me?

KITTY. Can I?

KITTY KITTY. Kiss me. *(They kiss. It's nice and sweet and tender. The clones notice.)*

KITTY KITTY KITTY KITTY. Who's that? *(They break up the kiss.)* Who's that?

KITTY. This is Kitty Kitty.

KITTY KITTY KITTY KITTY KITTY. *(Incomprehensible.)* [Who's Kitty Kitty?]

KITTY KITTY. *(To Kitty.)* What is he saying?

KITTY. *(To Kitty Kitty.)* He's a little slow. *(To Kitty Kitty Kitty Kitty Kitty.)* Kitty Kitty is the original of you.

BOTH CLONES. Original.

KITTY KITTY KITTY KITTY. What's original?

KITTY KITTY. Original: Middle English, from Old French, from Latin or-gin-alis, as an adjective: that from which a copy, reproduction, or translation is made. As a noun: a first form from which other forms are made or developed: *Later models of the car retained many features of the original.*

KITTY KITTY KITTY KITTY KITTY. [Can we fuck him?]

KITTY. No you cannot!

KITTY KITTY. What does he want?

KITTY. I'm afraid they want to have sex with you.

KITTY KITTY KITTY KITTY. Let's fuck the original!!! *(Kitty Kitty Kitty Kitty and Kitty Kitty Kitty Kitty Kitty approach Kitty Kitty. Kitty keeps them at bay.)*

KITTY. Stay away from him.

KITTY KITTY. I have to leave anyway.

KITTY. I can hold them back for a couple of minutes. Bad Kittys! Bad Kittys! *(Maybe he uses the spray bottle from before.)*

KITTY KITTY. I love you.

KITTY. I love you too. *(They kiss, the clones almost get him.)*

KITTY KITTY. Goodbye.

KITTY and CLONES. Goodbye. *(Kitty Kitty runs away.)*

BOTH CLONES. Goodbye! Goodbye! Goodbye!!!

KITTY. Look what you did! He could have stayed for a little longer. I hate you. I hate all of you! *(He hits them. Kitty Kitty Kitty Kitty starts coughing up blood.)*

KITTY KITTY KITTY KITTY. Blood. *(The others stand away from him.)*

KITTY. I'm sorry. I'm sorry. I didn't mean to hit you. I don't hate you. Please don't die. Don't leave me alone. *(The the next cat starts coughing. And the next. And the next. I forget how many there are total but they're all coughing up blood.)*

KITTY KITTY KITTY KITTY KITTY. *(Grunts and yells.)* [Blood.]

KITTY KITTY KITTY KITTY. Are we dying?

KITTY. Yes.

KITTY KITTY KITTY KITTY. Can you help us?

KITTY. I don't think so.

KITTY KITTY KITTY KITTY. Do you still love me?

KITTY. More than I can say.

KITTY KITTY KITTY KITTY KITTY. *(One last time, incomprehensible.)* [Do you still love me?]

KITTY. Yes. I love you, too. I love you all so very much. *(One by one they start dying. Just keeling over and dying. Not all at the same time. It's a one by one thing. So you've got a bunch of cat bodies on the ground. Kitty walks among them.)* Everything I ever loved is dead. Life is totally meaningless. If I committed suicide at the beginning I could have saved myself from so much pain. Oh well. Better late than never. *(Kitty picks up something and holds it to his throat. He's about to cut, when the Persons enter.)*

MR. PERSON. Excuse me?

KITTY. Yes, what is it?

MR. PERSON. Are you going to kill yourself?

KITTY. Yes, I am. How can you understand what I'm saying?

MR. PERSON. I took a class in "Communicating with your Cat" at the YMCA.

MRS. PERSON. We both did!

MR. PERSON. Why do you want to kill yourself?

KITTY. Because I'm really lonely.

MR. PERSON. Everyone's lonely.

MRS. PERSON. We're married and we're very lonely.

MR. PERSON. You get used to it.

KITTY. I don't want to get used to it.

MR. PERSON. Sometimes I'm happy.

MRS. PERSON. That's true. Sometimes we have fun.

KITTY. How often?

MR. PERSON. Not very often, but once in awhile.

KITTY. Like when was the last time?

MR. PERSON. Let's see.

MRS. PERSON. You were happy at dinner the other night.

MR. PERSON. Was I?

MRS. PERSON. You said you were.

MR. PERSON. I was lying.

MRS. PERSON. Oh.

MR. PERSON. I remember! It was with your clone. We were in the kitchen. I couldn't sleep.

MRS. PERSON. He never sleeps!

MR. PERSON. And when I pet him he purred so sweetly. And I forgot about everything for a minute or two. That made me happy.

KITTY. That's not enough for me. Goodbye.

MRS. PERSON. Wait!

KITTY. What?

MRS. PERSON. Would you like to come home and live with us?

KITTY. Live with you? You don't even know me.

MRS. PERSON. We loved your clone so much. How can we not love you?

KITTY. I'm different than him.

MR. PERSON. Of course you are. You're the original.

KITTY. That's right, I'm the original.

MR. PERSON. We'll find out all about you. We'll pay attention to your needs.

MRS. PERSON. We'll know what everything means.

MR. PERSON. Your smallest cries and whispers.

MRS. PERSON. Come live with us!

KITTY. I don't know. I've got so many terrible memories. So many regrets.

MR. PERSON. We'll make you forget all your regrets.

MRS. PERSON. We'll pamper you.

MR. PERSON. Bring you saucers of milk.

MRS. PERSON. Roll balls of twine for you to chase.

KITTY. I don't want to forget.

MR. PERSON. Then we'll help you remember. We'll stuff Sneakers' body and put it in front of the fireplace.

KITTY. Is that what you called him?

MRS. PERSON. His little white paws make it look like he's wearing a pair of sneakers. Just like yours.

KITTY. It's a good name.

MRS. PERSON. He seemed to take to it.

MR. PERSON. You loved him a lot?

KITTY. Yes, I did.

MR. PERSON. So did I.

MRS. PERSON. We all loved him!

MR. PERSON. We'll love you.

KITTY. You'll love me?

MR. PERSON. Yes.

KITTY. You'll love me forever?

MRS. PERSON. Forever and ever.

KITTY. Even if I scratch up the furniture?

MRS. PERSON. Yes.

KITTY. Even if I piss in the corners?

MR. PERSON. Yes.

KITTY. Even if I get on the dinner table when you've got guests over?

MR. PERSON. Unconditionally.

MRS. PERSON. Unconditionally.

KITTY. What will you name me?

MRS. PERSON. Whatever you want to be called.

KITTY. I like the name Sneakers.

MRS. PERSON. That'd be a little weird.

MR. PERSON. What about Sneakers the Second?

MRS. PERSON. What about Sneakers, Junior?

KITTY. How about Sneakers Sneakers?

MRS. PERSON. I like it.

MR. PERSON. Sneakers Sneakers it is, then.

MRS. PERSON. We're far from perfect but we'll try our best.

MR. PERSON. Will you come home with us, Sneakers Sneakers?

MRS. PERSON. Come home with us.

KITTY. Okay. Take me home. *(They all walk off together, careful to step over all of the dead bodies.)*

End of Play

PROPERTY LIST

Saucer of milk
Razor, shaving cream
Syringe
Cat treat
Towel, hair dryer
Camera
Spray bottle of water
Chew toy
Bottle
Ball of twine
Bowl of food, towel
Chains, padlocks
Cell phone
Flashlight
Pitch pipe

NEW PLAYS

★ **INTIMATE APPAREL by Lynn Nottage.** The moving and lyrical story of a turn-of-the-century black seamstress whose gifted hands and sewing machine are the tools she uses to fashion her dreams from the whole cloth of her life's experiences. "...Nottage's play has a delicacy and eloquence that seem absolutely right for the time she is depicting..." –*NY Daily News.* "...thoughtful, affecting...The play offers poignant commentary on an era when the cut and color of one's dress—and of course, skin—determined whom one could and could not marry, sleep with, even talk to in public." –*Variety.* [2M, 4W] ISBN: 0-8222-2009-1

★ **BROOKLYN BOY by Donald Margulies.** A witty and insightful look at what happens to a writer when his novel hits the bestseller list. "The characters are beautifully drawn, the dialogue sparkles..." –*nytheatre.com.* "Few playwrights have the mastery to smartly investigate so much through a laugh-out-loud comedy that combines the vintage subject matter of successful writer-returning-to-ethnic-roots with the familiar mid-life crisis." –*Show Business Weekly.* [4M, 3W] ISBN: 0-8222-2074-1

★ **CROWNS by Regina Taylor.** Hats become a springboard for an exploration of black history and identity in this celebratory musical play. "Taylor pulls off a Hat Trick: She scores thrice, turning CROWNS into an artful amalgamation of oral history, fashion show, and musical theater..." –*TheatreMania.com.* "...wholly theatrical...Ms. Taylor has created a show that seems to arise out of spontaneous combustion, as if a bevy of department-store customers simultaneously decided to stage a revival meeting in the changing room." –*NY Times.* [1M, 6W (2 musicians)] ISBN: 0-8222-1963-8

★ **EXITS AND ENTRANCES by Athol Fugard.** The story of a relationship between a young playwright on the threshold of his career and an aging actor who has reached the end of his. "[Fugard] can say more with a single line than most playwrights convey in an entire script...Paraphrasing the title, it's safe to say this drama, making its memorable entrance into our consciousness, is unlikely to exit as long as a theater exists for exceptional work." –*Variety.* "A thought-provoking, elegant and engrossing new play..." –*Hollywood Reporter.* [2M] ISBN: 0-8222-2041-5

★ **BUG by Tracy Letts.** A thriller featuring a pair of star-crossed lovers in an Oklahoma City motel facing a bug invasion, paranoia, conspiracy theories and twisted psychological motives. "...obscenely exciting...top-flight craftsmanship. Buckle up and brace yourself..." –*NY Times.* "...[a] thoroughly outrageous and thoroughly entertaining play...the possibility of enemies, real and imagined, to squash has never been more theatrical." –*A.P.* [3M, 2W] ISBN: 0-8222-2016-4

★ **THOM PAIN (BASED ON NOTHING) by Will Eno.** An ordinary man muses on childhood, yearning, disappointment and loss, as he draws the audience into his last-ditch plea for empathy and enlightenment. "It's one of those treasured nights in the theater—treasured nights anywhere, for that matter—that can leave you both breathless with exhilaration and...in a puddle of tears." –*NY Times.* "Eno's words...are familiar, but proffered in a way that is constantly contradictory to our expectations. Beckett is certainly among his literary ancestors." –*nytheatre.com.* [1M] ISBN: 0-8222-2076-8

★ **THE LONG CHRISTMAS RIDE HOME by Paula Vogel.** Past, present and future collide on a snowy Christmas Eve for a troubled family of five. "...[a] lovely and hauntingly original family drama...a work that breathes so much life into the theater." –*Time Out.* "...[a] delicate visual feast..." –*NY Times.* "...brutal and lovely...the overall effect is magical." –*NY Newsday.* [3M, 3W] ISBN: 0-8222-2003-2

DRAMATISTS PLAY SERVICE, INC.
440 Park Avenue South, New York, NY 10016 212-683-8960 Fax 212-213-1539
postmaster@dramatists.com www.dramatists.com